Table of Contents

Introduction..1
Chapter 1: Introduction to the Music Lessons Business..3
Chapter 2: Assessing Your Musical Skills and Qualifications...6
Chapter 3: Understanding Your Target Market.10
Chapter 4: Developing Your Curriculum and Lesson Plans..14
Chapter 5: Setting Up Your Teaching Space....18
Chapter 6: Legal and Business Considerations.. 23
Chapter 7: Marketing and Promotion Strategies. 28
Chapter 8: Acquiring Students and Building Relationships...33
Chapter 9: Providing Exceptional Instruction and Support..38
Chapter 10: Growing Your Music Lessons Business...43

Introduction

Welcome to "The Ultimate Guide on How To Start a Music Lessons Business." This guide is packed with comprehensive insights and practical advice designed to help you establish and grow your own music lessons business. Whether you're a seasoned musician eager to share your knowledge or an aspiring entrepreneur ready to dive into the lucrative world of music instruction, this guide has got you covered.

Starting a music lessons business is a rewarding endeavor. It allows you to make a positive impact on your students' lives while also pursuing your own musical interests. However, success in this competitive industry requires careful planning, effective marketing, and exceptional teaching skills.

Throughout this guide, we'll walk you through the essential steps to set up and run a thriving music lessons business. By the end, you'll have a solid understanding of how to:

- Assess your skills and qualifications.
- Identify your target market.
- Develop engaging curricula and lesson plans.
- Create an ideal teaching space.
- Navigate legal and business considerations.
- Implement effective marketing strategies.
- Acquire and retain students.
- Provide exceptional instruction and support.

Whether you decide to specialize in piano, guitar, singing, or a combination of these disciplines, the principles outlined in this guide apply to all music lessons businesses. Feel free to adapt the strategies to fit your specific needs and goals to ensure your success.

Now, let's embark on this exciting journey together and uncover the ins and outs of starting and growing your own music lessons business!

Chapter 1: Introduction to the Music Lessons Business

Starting a music lessons business can be an exciting and rewarding venture, especially if you have a deep passion for music and teaching. In this chapter, we'll delve into the basics of the music lessons industry, helping you build a solid foundation to get your business started on the right note.

Understanding the Music Lessons Industry

Before we get into the nitty-gritty of launching your own music lessons business, it's crucial to grasp the broader picture of the industry. Over the years, the music education sector has seen continuous growth, with an increasing number of people recognizing the immense value of learning to play an instrument or refining their vocal skills. From young children to adults, music lovers of all ages seek out professional instruction to develop their musical abilities. Whether it's mastering the piano, strumming a guitar, or perfecting vocal techniques, there's a steady demand for qualified teachers who can inspire and guide students on their musical journeys.

Benefits of Starting a Music Lessons Business

Starting a music lessons business comes with a host of benefits that make it a truly rewarding endeavor. First and foremost, it gives you the chance to share your love and knowledge of music with others, making a significant positive impact on their lives. There's something incredibly fulfilling about watching your students progress and achieve their musical goals.

Running your own music lessons business also offers a level of flexibility and independence that's hard to beat. You get to set your own hours, choose your teaching methods, and design a curriculum that reflects your values and expertise. Plus, there's considerable potential for financial success, especially if you build a solid reputation and attract a steady stream of students. Over time, your dedication and passion can translate into a thriving and profitable business.

Challenges and Considerations

Of course, every business comes with its challenges, and a music lessons business is no exception. One of the primary hurdles you might face is competition, particularly in saturated markets. Standing out from the crowd will require a unique approach and a strong personal brand. Additionally, consistently attracting and retaining students demands effective marketing strategies and exceptional teaching skills.

Legal and business considerations are equally important. You'll need to understand local regulations, obtain the necessary licenses and permits, and ensure you have proper insurance coverage. These elements are crucial to running a legitimate and successful business, so it's vital to address them early on.

The Objective of This Book

The purpose of this book is to guide aspiring music entrepreneurs like yourself through the process of starting a music lessons business successfully. We'll cover a wide range of topics, including assessing your musical skills, identifying your target market, developing a comprehensive curriculum, setting up your teaching space, handling legal and business matters, implementing marketing strategies, acquiring students, and providing exceptional instruction and support.

By the time you finish this book, you'll have a clear understanding of what it takes to launch and grow a thriving music lessons business. So, let's embark on this exciting journey together and turn your passion for music into a profitable and fulfilling venture. Stay tuned for the next chapter: "Assessing Your Musical Skills and Qualifications."

Chapter 2: Assessing Your Musical Skills and Qualifications

Starting a music lessons business is an exciting venture, but before diving in, it's essential to take a good look at your own musical skills and qualifications. This self-assessment not only helps you figure out what type of lessons you can offer but also boosts your confidence and credibility as a music instructor. In this chapter, we'll walk through various ways to effectively assess your musical skills and qualifications.

Evaluating Your Musical Skills

To teach others, you first need to have a clear understanding of your own abilities. This self-evaluation helps you pinpoint your strengths and identify areas that might need a bit more work. Here are some ways to get started:

Self-Assessment

Start by being honest with yourself about your musical abilities. Make a list of the instruments you can play well, your level of expertise on each one, and any additional musical skills or knowledge you have. Recognize your strong points and the genres you excel in, as well as areas where you could improve.

Musical Education and Training

Think about your formal musical education and training. Have you taken any music courses or earned a music degree? Assess the level of training you've received and note any certifications or qualifications you have. These credentials will enhance your credibility and attract potential students.

Performance Experience

Consider your performance experience. Have you played in bands, performed at concerts, or taken part in any musical events? Reflect on the venues where you've performed and the size of the audiences you've entertained. Performance experience shows that you can effectively showcase your musical talent.

Feedback and Recommendations

Seek feedback and recommendations from trusted sources, like music instructors, fellow musicians, or industry professionals. They can provide an external perspective on your musical skills and qualifications. Constructive feedback can highlight areas for improvement and guide your learning journey.

Identifying Your Teaching Abilities

Assessing your teaching abilities is just as important as evaluating your musical skills. Teaching others requires a unique set of skills and qualifications. Here's how to identify your teaching strengths:

Communication Skills

Effective communication is key in any teaching profession. Consider your ability to explain and demonstrate musical concepts clearly. Reflect on any experience you have in teaching others, whether it's through private tutoring, volunteering, or leading group classes.

Patience and Empathy

Teaching music can be challenging, especially when students struggle. Assess your patience and empathy towards learners of different musical abilities. Recognize the importance of maintaining a positive and encouraging learning environment for your students.

Adaptability and Flexibility

Evaluate your ability to adapt and tailor your teaching methods to meet the needs and learning styles of your students. A good music teacher can customize lesson plans, provide individualized instruction, and adjust the pace of learning to ensure maximum student engagement and progress.

Passion for Teaching

A genuine passion for teaching is crucial. Reflect on your enthusiasm for sharing knowledge and helping others grow musically. A true passion for teaching will make your lessons more engaging and enjoyable for your students.

Setting Goals for Improvement

Once you've assessed your musical skills and teaching abilities, it's important to set goals for improvement. Identify areas where you can expand your musical knowledge and skills. Consider taking advanced music lessons, attending workshops or masterclasses, or seeking mentorship from experienced musicians or teachers. Remember, continuous self-improvement is crucial for any music instructor. As you expand your own musical abilities, you'll be better equipped to provide exceptional instruction to your students.

In the next chapter, we'll dive into understanding your target market and how it can impact your music lessons business.

Chapter 3: Understanding Your Target Market

So, you've decided to start a music lessons business—fantastic! But before you can hit the right notes with your students, it's crucial to really understand who your audience is. In other words, you need to know your target market inside and out. This chapter will walk you through the process of identifying and analyzing the specific group of people most likely to be interested in your music lessons.

Identifying Your Target Market

First things first, let's figure out who would benefit the most from your music lessons and who would be willing to pay for them. Begin by defining the demographic characteristics of your target market. Think about age, gender, income level, and location. Are you aiming to teach kids, adults, or perhaps both? Maybe you want to focus on beginners or advanced students. Narrowing down these details will help you tailor your approach.

Next, dive into the psychographic characteristics of your target market. This is about understanding their interests, values, lifestyles, and motivations. Ask yourself: Are these aspiring musicians dreaming of a career in music, or are they hobbyists wanting to play for fun? Understanding their needs and desires will allow you to design lessons that resonate with them personally.

Market Research

Once you have a clear idea of who your target market is, it's time to gather some detailed information through market research. This can be done in a variety of ways, such as surveys, interviews, or focus groups with potential customers.

When conducting market research, ask questions that will help you get a better picture of their musical backgrounds, goals, and preferences. For instance, you might ask about their previous musical training, favorite music genres, and the specific instruments they want to learn. These insights will be invaluable in customizing your curriculum and lesson plans to fit their needs perfectly.

Competitor Analysis

Understanding your target market is only one piece of the puzzle. You also need to know what other music lessons providers in your area are up to. Conduct a competitor analysis to see what they offer, how they market their services, and what their pricing structures look like.

By analyzing your competitors, you can identify gaps in the market and find unique selling points for your business. Perhaps there's a particular style of music or a type of lesson format that's underrepresented. Use this information to set yourself apart and attract more customers.

Creating a Customer Persona

To make all this information more actionable, it's helpful to create a customer persona. A customer persona is a fictional representation of your ideal customer based on the data you've gathered. Give your persona a name, age, occupation, and other relevant details.

For example, you might create "Sarah," a 35-year-old graphic designer who loves jazz and wants to learn the saxophone in her spare time. Whenever you make business decisions—whether it's designing promotional materials or developing new lesson plans—refer back to Sarah. This will keep your efforts aligned with the needs and interests of your target market.

Bringing It All Together

By thoroughly understanding your target market, conducting thorough market research, analyzing competitors, and creating a detailed customer persona, you'll be in a strong position to tailor your music lessons business to your ideal customers. This approach will not only help you attract and retain students but also ensure they are satisfied and likely to recommend your services to others.

Remember, the key to a successful music lessons business isn't just about being a great teacher—it's about connecting with your students and meeting their unique needs. With a clear understanding of your target market, you'll be well on your way to hitting all the right notes in your business.

Chapter 4: Developing Your Curriculum and Lesson Plans

Developing a well-structured curriculum and lesson plans is crucial for running a successful music lessons business. Think of your curriculum as a roadmap for your students' musical journey, providing them with a clear progression and helping them build their skills step by step. In this chapter, we'll explore the key factors to consider when developing your curriculum and lesson plans to ensure your students get the most out of their lessons.

Define Your Learning Objectives

Before diving into creating your curriculum, it's important to define your learning objectives. What specific goals do you want your students to achieve? Are you aiming for them to learn a particular musical style, master certain techniques, or prepare for music exams? Clearly outlining your learning objectives will guide you in structuring your curriculum and lesson plans effectively.

Break Down the Content

Once you've defined your learning objectives, the next step is to break them down into smaller, manageable units. For example, if one of your goals is for students to learn chords on the guitar, you might break this down into individual major and minor chords, barre chords, and chord progressions. By breaking down the content, you can organize it in a logical and progressive manner, making it easier for your students to follow and understand.

Sequence the Lessons

After breaking down the content, it's time to sequence the lessons in a way that ensures optimal learning progression. Start with the foundational concepts and gradually introduce more complex topics. For instance, in piano lessons, you might begin with finger exercises and basic scales before moving on to advanced techniques like chord inversions and improvisation. Sequencing the lessons in this manner helps students build a strong foundation before tackling more challenging material.

Incorporate Variety

Keeping your lessons engaging and varied is essential for maintaining your students' interest and motivation. Incorporate a mix of theory, technique exercises, song learning, improvisation, and ear training activities. Variety not only keeps lessons enjoyable, but it also helps students develop a well-rounded musical skill set. Remember, a bored student is less likely to stay motivated and continue their lessons.

Personalize for Individual Students

Each student is unique, with their own strengths, weaknesses, and musical goals. As a music instructor, it's essential to personalize your curriculum and lesson plans to meet each student's needs. Consider their musical preferences, learning style, and pace of progress. Tailoring the lessons to individual students maximizes their learning potential and keeps them motivated. For example, if a student loves jazz, try to incorporate jazz pieces and techniques into their lessons.

Allow Room for Flexibility

While having a well-structured curriculum is important, it's also crucial to leave room for flexibility. Students may have specific requests, interests, or areas they want to focus on. Being adaptable and open to incorporating their suggestions will enhance their overall learning experience and keep them engaged in the lessons. Flexibility also allows you to adjust your teaching approach based on the student's progress and feedback.

Continuously Evaluate and Update

Curriculum development is an ongoing process. As you gain more teaching experience and receive feedback from students, continuously evaluate and update your curriculum and lesson plans. Seek feedback from your students to understand what is working well and what might need improvement. Stay up-to-date with new techniques, teaching resources, and industry trends to ensure your curriculum remains relevant and effective.

Conclusion

Developing a comprehensive curriculum and lesson plans is a vital aspect of starting a music lessons business. By defining your objectives, breaking down the content, sequencing lessons, incorporating variety, personalizing for individual students, allowing flexibility, and continuously evaluating and updating, you'll be well-equipped to provide high-quality music instruction and meet the needs of your students. In the next chapter, we will discuss how to set up your teaching space to create a conducive learning environment for your students.

Chapter 5: Setting Up Your Teaching Space

Starting a music lessons business is an exciting venture, but one of the key steps is creating a comfortable and conducive learning environment for your students. The setting of your teaching space can significantly impact the overall experience and effectiveness of your lessons. Let's delve into the key considerations and steps to set up your ideal teaching space.

Assessing Your Space Requirements

Before you dive into arranging your teaching space, it's essential to evaluate what specific requirements you'll need based on the type of music lessons you offer. Different instruments, like the piano, guitar, or vocals, will have varying spatial needs and equipment. Here are some important factors to consider:

Size: First, determine the size of the space you need to comfortably accommodate both yourself and your students. Make sure there's ample room for movement and enough space for the instrument(s) and any necessary equipment. You don't want your students feeling cramped or restricted.

Acoustics: Next, pay close attention to the acoustics of your teaching space. It's important that the space is well-insulated to minimize disturbances from external noises. Think about the type of flooring, wall materials, and soundproofing options to ensure optimal sound quality during lessons. Good acoustics can make a big difference in the learning experience.

Lighting: Good lighting is essential for creating a conducive learning environment. Natural light is always the best option, but if that's not feasible, make sure you have adequate artificial lighting that doesn't cause strain or cast shadows on the instrument or sheet music. Proper lighting helps in keeping the students focused and engaged.

Ergonomics: Ensure that the seating arrangement and positioning of the instruments are ergonomically sound. Students should be able to maintain a comfortable posture while playing or singing to reduce the risk of physical strain or injuries. Ergonomic considerations can enhance the comfort and performance of your students.

Choosing Instruments and Equipment

The choice of instruments and equipment is crucial in setting up a well-equipped teaching space. Here are some factors to keep in mind:

Instruments: Ensure you have high-quality instruments available for your students to use during lessons. Depending on your expertise and the type of lessons you offer, you might need pianos, guitars, microphones, amplifiers, and other musical instruments. Invest in instruments that are well-maintained and in good working condition to provide the best learning experience.

Music Stands: Music stands are essential for holding sheet music or instructional materials during lessons. It's recommended to have adjustable music stands that can be positioned at a suitable height for each student. This flexibility can accommodate the varying needs of your students.

Reference Materials: Arrange your teaching space with a variety of reference materials such as music theory books, songbooks, sheet music collections, and other educational resources. These materials can support your teaching and provide additional learning opportunities for your students.

Technology: Consider incorporating technology into your teaching space. This can include audio recording equipment, metronomes, tuners, video lesson recording devices, or music software that enhances the learning experience. Technology can be a great tool to make lessons more interactive and engaging.

Creating a Welcoming Atmosphere

Beyond the physical setup, creating a welcoming atmosphere is vital for promoting a positive and engaging learning experience. Here are some tips to help you achieve this:

Aesthetics: Decorate your teaching space with visual elements that inspire creativity and a passion for music. Use tasteful artwork, inspirational quotes, or musical symbols to create a visually appealing environment. Aesthetically pleasing surroundings can boost motivation and creativity.

Comfort: Ensure the seating arrangements and temperature in your teaching space are comfortable for both you and your students. Consider adding cushions or ergonomic seating options and regulate the temperature to a pleasant level. Comfort plays a key role in maintaining focus and concentration during lessons.

Cleanliness: Maintain cleanliness in your teaching space by regularly cleaning and organizing the area. A clean and clutter-free environment helps students stay focused and feel more comfortable. It also reflects professionalism and care on your part.

Personal Touch: Add personal touches to your teaching space that reflect your musical journey and personality. Displaying your musical accomplishments or showcasing the instruments you play can help establish a connection with your students. Personal touches can make the space feel warm and inviting.

Conclusion

Setting up your teaching space involves careful consideration of the physical requirements, instruments, equipment, and the creation of a welcoming atmosphere. By creating a comfortable and conducive learning environment, you are setting the stage for successful music lessons. In the next chapter, we will explore the legal and business considerations related to starting a music lessons business.

So, stay tuned as we dive into the important aspects of running your music lessons business smoothly and effectively.

Chapter 6: Legal and Business Considerations

Starting a music lessons business is an exciting endeavor, but there's more to it than just teaching music. To ensure your business runs smoothly and successfully, it's crucial to understand the legal and business aspects involved. This chapter will guide you through the important considerations you need to keep in mind.

Business Structure

One of the first steps in starting your music lessons business is deciding on the legal structure that best suits your needs. The most common business structures are sole proprietorship, partnership, limited liability company (LLC), and corporation. Each of these structures has its own set of advantages and disadvantages in terms of liability, taxes, and management.

For example, a sole proprietorship is simple to set up and gives you complete control over your business, but it also means you're personally liable for all business debts. An LLC, on the other hand, offers some protection from personal liability while still allowing for flexible management.

It's a good idea to consult with a business attorney or an accountant to determine the most suitable structure for your music lessons business. They can provide valuable guidance on the legal requirements and tax obligations associated with each structure.

Business Permits and Licenses

Depending on where you live, you may need to obtain certain permits and licenses to operate your music lessons business legally. These requirements can vary greatly from one country to another, and even from state to state. Some common permits and licenses you might need include a business license, a music teaching license, and zoning permits.

To ensure you comply with all legal requirements, research the specific regulations in your area. Contact your local government offices or visit their websites to gather information about the necessary permits and licenses. It's better to be thorough now than to face legal issues later.

Insurance

Insurance is a crucial consideration for any business, including a music lessons business. Protecting yourself, your students, and your assets from potential risks and liabilities is essential.

Consider obtaining liability insurance to cover any accidents, injuries, or property damage that might occur during your lessons. An insurance agent who specializes in small businesses can help you identify the most suitable insurance coverage for your needs. They can guide you through different insurance options and ensure that you have adequate protection for your business.

Contracts and Policies

Having clear and well-drafted contracts and policies in place is important for protecting your business and setting guidelines for your students and their parents. Develop a contract that outlines the terms and conditions of your lessons, including payment terms, cancellation policies, and expectations for both parties.

Consider creating policies regarding scheduling, attendance, practice requirements, and a code of conduct. These policies help ensure that everyone involved understands their responsibilities and expectations, which can prevent misunderstandings and disputes down the line.

Financial Management

Proper financial management is crucial for the success of your music lessons business. Keep accurate records of your income and expenses, including tuition payments, instrument purchases, and operating costs. This practice will help you keep track of your business's financial health and ensure compliance with tax regulations.

Consider using accounting software or hiring a professional bookkeeper to help you manage your finances effectively. Additionally, consult with a tax professional to understand your tax obligations and ensure that you are complying with all applicable laws.

Copyright and Music Licensing

As a music instructor, it's important to respect copyright laws and obtain the necessary licenses for any copyrighted materials you use in your lessons. If you provide sheet music, recordings, or other copyrighted materials to your students, make sure you have the appropriate permissions or licenses to distribute them.

Research the copyright laws in your country and consult with a legal professional specializing in intellectual property to ensure that you are compliant with all copyright regulations. This diligence not only protects you legally but also supports the artists and creators whose work you use.

Conclusion

Understanding and addressing the legal and business considerations of running a music lessons business is crucial for its success. From choosing the right business structure to obtaining permits and licenses, managing insurance, and implementing contracts and policies, taking care of these aspects will help you operate smoothly and protect your interests.

Seek professional advice when necessary to ensure compliance with all relevant laws and regulations. With these foundational pieces in place, you can focus on what you love most: teaching music. In the next chapter, we will explore various marketing and promotion strategies to attract potential students and grow your music lessons business.

Chapter 7: Marketing and Promotion Strategies

Marketing and promotion are the lifeblood of any successful business, and your music lessons venture is no exception. To attract students and build a strong customer base, you need to employ a variety of effective strategies. Let's dive into some of the best ways to market and promote your music lessons business.

1. Create a Professional Brand

In the crowded world of music lessons, having a standout professional brand is crucial. This means crafting an identity that showcases your expertise and the unique value you bring. Start with a compelling brand identity—think about a memorable logo, a cohesive color scheme, and visual elements that will resonate with your target market. Your brand should be consistent and recognizable, setting you apart from the competition.

2. Develop a Strong Online Presence

In today's digital era, a strong online presence is non-negotiable. Begin by creating a professional website that highlights everything potential students need to know—your music lessons, instructor profiles, testimonials, and contact details. Make sure your website is optimized for search engines to boost its visibility.

Social media is another powerful tool. Establish profiles on platforms like Facebook, Instagram, and YouTube. Regularly post engaging content—tips, tutorials, and performance videos—to attract potential students and build a following. Encourage your current students to share their experiences and recommend your lessons on social media. This can significantly extend your reach.

3. Utilize Online Directories and Review Platforms

Listing your business on online directories like Yelp, Google My Business, and music lesson-specific platforms can greatly enhance your visibility. These platforms are frequented by people actively searching for music lessons. Encourage your satisfied customers to leave positive reviews. Good reviews build credibility and can improve your ranking in search results, making it easier for new students to find you.

4. Offer Promotions and Incentives

Who doesn't love a good deal? Attract new students and encourage repeat business by offering promotions and incentives. Consider discounted trial lessons, referral discounts, or package deals for multiple lessons. These offers can be the nudge that potential students need to choose your music lessons over others.

5. Collaborate with Local Schools and Community Organizations

Building partnerships with local schools, community organizations, and music-related businesses can be incredibly beneficial. Offer to host workshops or informational sessions on the benefits of music education at local schools or community centers. Partnering with music stores or instrument manufacturers can also lead to mutual referrals and promotional opportunities, broadening your reach in the community.

6. Advertise in Local Media

Don't underestimate the power of traditional media. Advertise your music lessons in local newspapers, magazines, radio stations, and online platforms. Focus on publications that cater to your target demographic and use catchy headlines and compelling visuals to grab attention. Local events and festivals are also great opportunities to distribute flyers or promotional materials.

7. Build Relationships with Local Teachers and Musicians

Networking with local teachers and musicians can open up a world of opportunities. Attend local music events, workshops, and conferences to meet other professionals in your field. Collaborate on projects, refer students to one another, and share resources. These relationships can help expand your network and attract more students.

8. Leverage the Power of Word-of-Mouth

One of the most effective marketing tools is positive word-of-mouth. Provide exceptional instruction and ensure your students have a great experience. Happy students are likely to recommend your lessons to friends, family, and colleagues. Consider offering referral discounts to incentivize students to spread the word about your business.

9. Monitor and Track Your Marketing Efforts

To ensure your marketing strategies are working, it's vital to monitor and track your efforts. Use analytics tools to measure website traffic, social media engagement, and conversion rates. This data will give you valuable insights into which strategies are effective and which ones might need tweaking.

10. Continuously Adapt and Evolve

The marketing landscape is always changing, so staying flexible and adaptive is key. Keep up with new marketing trends and techniques. Regularly seek feedback from your students and evaluate the success of your marketing efforts. Adjust your strategies as needed to ensure you're effectively reaching your target market.

By implementing these marketing and promotion strategies, you'll be well on your way to attracting students and building a successful music lessons business. Remember, the keys to long-term success are consistency, creativity, and a deep understanding of your target market. Happy teaching!

Chapter 8: Acquiring Students and Building Relationships

Running a successful music lessons business isn't just about getting students through the door; it's also about building strong, lasting relationships with them. In this chapter, we'll dive into various strategies to attract new students and create meaningful connections that will keep them coming back.

Develop a Marketing Plan

Before you can start acquiring students, it's essential to have a well-defined marketing plan. This begins with clearly identifying your target market and understanding their needs and preferences. Knowing who you're trying to reach will help you tailor your marketing efforts effectively.

Online Marketing Tactics

Creating an Engaging Website: Your website is often the first impression potential students will have of your business, so make it count. Invest in a professionally designed website that showcases your expertise, accomplishments, testimonials, and contact information. Ensure your site is visually appealing, easy to navigate, and mobile-friendly.

Utilizing Social Media Platforms: Social media is a powerful tool for promoting your music lessons.

Create engaging content that highlights your teaching style, student success stories, and upcoming events. Engage with your audience by responding to comments and messages promptly. Consider running targeted advertisements to reach a broader audience.

Offline Marketing Tactics

Offering Referral Incentives: Encourage your current students to refer their friends and family to your music lessons by offering incentives such as discounts or free lessons. Word-of-mouth referrals can be incredibly powerful in attracting new students.

Networking and Collaborations: Attend local music events, conferences, and workshops to connect with fellow musicians, teachers, and industry professionals. Collaborate with them on projects, workshops, or performances to expand your network and reach new potential students.

Provide Exceptional Customer Service

Getting students is only the first step; keeping them and building a positive relationship is equally important. Providing exceptional customer service not only improves the overall experience for your students but also encourages their loyalty and positive word-of-mouth.

Tips for Exceptional Customer Service

Communicate Clearly and Promptly: Respond to inquiries, emails, and phone calls in a timely manner. Be clear and concise in your communication, addressing any questions or concerns. Establishing prompt and effective communication will set a great impression from the start.

Personalize the Learning Experience: Each student is unique, with different goals, learning styles, and preferences. Take the time to understand your students' individual needs and personalize their lessons accordingly. This shows them that you genuinely care about their progress and makes their lessons more effective and enjoyable.

Encourage Feedback and Continuous Improvement: Regularly seek feedback from your students to understand their satisfaction level and areas for improvement. Actively listen to their suggestions and make adjustments to your teaching methods or curriculum as needed. By continuously improving your teaching and addressing student needs, you will enhance their learning experience.

Foster a Sense of Community

Creating a sense of community within your music lessons business can greatly enhance student retention and encourage positive word-of-mouth referrals. Encourage collaboration and interaction among your students to build connections and a supportive learning environment.

Building a Community

Organize Recitals and Performances: Regularly organize recitals or performances where your students can showcase their progress and gain confidence. This provides a platform for students to connect with and support one another. It also allows parents, friends, and family members to celebrate their achievements.

Establish Online Forums or Groups: Create online forums or groups where students can interact, ask questions, and share their musical journey. Encourage participation and facilitate discussions to foster a sense of camaraderie and support among your students.

Offer Group Lessons or Workshops: In addition to individual lessons, consider offering group lessons or workshops where students can learn together and collaborate. This not only provides a more affordable option for some students but also allows them to learn from their peers and build connections.

Building strong relationships with your students is essential for the long-term success of your music lessons business. By implementing effective marketing strategies, providing exceptional customer service, and fostering a sense of community, you can attract new students and cultivate lasting connections that will contribute to the growth and reputation of your business.

In the next chapter, we will discuss the importance of providing exceptional instruction and support to ensure the success of your students.

Chapter 9: Providing Exceptional Instruction and Support

Exceptional instruction and support are crucial factors in running a successful music lessons business. As a music instructor, your primary goal is to help your students develop their musical skills and achieve their goals. This chapter will explore various strategies and techniques to provide exceptional instruction and support to your students.

Tailoring Lessons to Individual Students

Each student is unique, with different learning styles, goals, and abilities. It's essential to tailor your lessons to meet their individual needs. Let's look at some effective strategies for doing this:

Assessing Student's Skill Level and Goals

Before you start lessons with a new student, take the time to assess their current skill level and goals. This assessment will help you understand their strengths, weaknesses, and aspirations. By knowing where they are and where they want to go, you can customize your teaching approach to suit them perfectly.

Adapting Teaching Techniques

Modify your teaching techniques to match the learning style of each student. Some students respond better to visual aids, while others prefer hands-on activities or audio-based learning. By adapting your methods, you can ensure that students grasp the concepts effectively and enjoy the learning process.

Setting Realistic and Attainable Goals

Help your students set realistic and attainable goals. Break down their long-term goals into smaller, manageable milestones. This approach will keep them motivated and engaged, as they will experience a sense of progress and accomplishment at each stage of their musical journey.

Creating a Positive and Motivating Learning Environment

Creating a positive and motivating learning environment is vital for student engagement and progress. Here are some strategies to foster such an environment:

Encouraging and Positive Feedback

Offer regular feedback to your students, emphasizing their strengths and areas for improvement. Constructive criticism should be delivered positively and encouragingly. Celebrate their achievements, no matter how small, to boost their confidence and motivation.

Fostering a Supportive Community

Encourage a sense of community among your students. Organize group lessons, workshops, or recitals where students can interact, collaborate, and learn from each other. This sense of camaraderie will create a supportive and motivating environment for all participants.

Providing Resources and Support Materials

Offer a variety of resources and support materials to your students. This can include sheet music, practice exercises, online tutorials, or recommended recordings. By providing these resources, you empower your students to continue their learning outside of the classroom and explore different musical styles and genres.

Continued Professional Development

As a music instructor, it's crucial to continually improve your own skills and knowledge to provide the best instruction and support. Here are some strategies to consider:

Attend Workshops and Conferences

Participate in workshops, conferences, or seminars related to music education. These events provide opportunities to learn from experts in the field, gain new insights, and explore innovative teaching techniques.

Collaborate with Peers

Collaborate with fellow music instructors and exchange ideas and strategies. Join professional organizations or online communities to connect with like-minded individuals and engage in discussions about music education.

Seek Feedback and Self-Reflect

Regularly seek feedback from your students, their parents, or fellow instructors. Reflect on your teaching methods, strengths, and areas for improvement. Incorporate this feedback into your teaching practices to enhance your instructional abilities.

Continuing Education

Consider pursuing further education or certifications in music education or related fields. This additional credentialing will not only enhance your knowledge but also help build credibility and trust among potential students.

Conclusion

Remember, exceptional instruction and support are the foundations of a successful music lessons business. By tailoring lessons to individual needs, creating a positive learning environment, and investing in your own professional development, you can provide your students with an exceptional learning experience that will keep them motivated and dedicated to their musical journey. With dedication and the right approach, you can inspire your students to reach their full potential and enjoy the wonderful world of music.

Chapter 10: Growing Your Music Lessons Business

Growing your music lessons business is crucial for its long-term success and sustainability. As you establish a solid foundation and gain traction in your local market, it's essential to focus on expansion and attracting new students. In this chapter, we'll delve into various strategies and techniques to help you grow your music lessons business effectively.

1. Expand Your Offerings

One effective way to attract more students and grow your business is by diversifying your offerings. Instead of sticking solely to traditional piano, guitar, and singing lessons, consider introducing new instruments or specialized courses. Think about offering lessons for the violin, drums, or even niche instruments like the ukulele or mandolin. Additionally, you could introduce group lessons, advanced masterclasses, or workshops to cater to different learning preferences and interests. This variety not only appeals to a broader audience but also showcases your versatility as a music instructor.

2. Foster Partnerships and Collaborations

Collaborating with local schools, community centers, or other music-related businesses can significantly expand your reach and attract new students. Reach out to these institutions and explore opportunities for joint promotional events, performances, or workshops. Leveraging the existing networks of these organizations can increase your visibility and credibility within the community.

Furthermore, consider partnering with local musicians or music teachers who specialize in different instruments or styles. This collaboration can help you cross-promote each other's services and expand your customer base. Imagine hosting a joint recital or a summer music camp—it's a fantastic way to draw in students from various backgrounds.

3. Utilize Online Marketing Strategies

In today's digital age, having a strong online presence is crucial for the growth of any business. Start by developing a professional website that showcases your services, highlights your expertise, and provides an easy way for potential students to contact you. Optimize your website for search engines to increase its visibility and attract organic traffic.

In addition to a website, leverage social media platforms to engage with your audience and promote your music lessons business. Create compelling content, such as tutorials, performance videos, or student success stories, and share them on platforms like Facebook, Instagram, and YouTube. Social media advertising can help you reach a wider audience and target specific demographics.

Consider investing in online directory listings and review platforms specific to music lessons. These platforms can boost your visibility and credibility, as potential students often rely on recommendations and reviews when choosing a music instructor. Encourage satisfied students to leave positive reviews to build a strong online reputation.

4. Offer Referral Incentives

Word-of-mouth referrals are a powerful and cost-effective way to attract new students. Encourage your current students and their parents to refer their friends, family, and acquaintances to your music lessons business. Incentivize this referral behavior by offering discounts, rewards, or free lessons to both the referring student and the new student they bring in. This creates a win-win situation and motivates your existing students to actively promote your business.

5. Attend Music Conferences and Workshops

Continuously expanding your knowledge and skills as a music instructor is crucial for the growth of your business. Attend music conferences, workshops, and seminars to network with fellow professionals, learn about the latest teaching techniques, and stay updated on industry trends. These events provide valuable educational opportunities and offer a chance to promote your business and make connections that can lead to future collaborations or referrals.

6. Provide Exceptional Customer Service

Exceptional customer service is key to retaining existing students and attracting new ones. Ensure that you provide prompt and clear communication to potential and current students. Be responsive to inquiries, address concerns promptly, and maintain a positive and supportive attitude throughout the student journey.

Personalize the learning experience by understanding and catering to each student's unique needs, goals, and learning styles. Offering resources, practice tips, and ongoing support outside of lesson times can also enhance the student experience and promote loyalty. Going the extra mile in customer service can turn your students into enthusiastic advocates for your business.

Conclusion

Growing your music lessons business requires strategic planning, continuous effort, and a focus on providing an exceptional learning experience. By expanding your offerings, fostering partnerships, utilizing online marketing strategies, offering referral incentives, attending music conferences, and providing outstanding customer service, you can attract new students and ensure the long-term success of your music lessons business.

Remember to continually evaluate and refine your growth strategies based on market feedback and evolving industry trends. With determination and dedication, you can build a thriving and profitable music lessons business that stands the test of time.

www.ingramcontent.com/pod-product-compliance
Lightning Source LLC
Chambersburg PA
CBHW070138230526
45472CB00004B/1583